Music City's Showcase

THE TENNESSEAN

IMAGES

To purchase images that appear in this book, see http://Tennessean.com/purchasephotos and include the book's title in the description of the photo; or in the United States call 1-877-843-2900.

REPRINTS

To reprint or republish portions of this book, contact PARS International, http://www.gannettreprints.com or call 1-212-221-9595, ext. 116.

ON THE COVER: Traffic cruises past Music City Center on the evening of May 2, 2013, just weeks before the grand opening of Nashville's much anticipated convention complex. DIPTI VAIDYA

MUSIC CITY'S SHOWCASE

Copyright © 2013 by The Tennessean. All rights reserved.

Published by The Tennessean, Nashville, TN

All rights reserved. No part of this publication may be reproduced or transmitted in any form or by any means, electronic or mechanical, including photocopying or recording, or by any information storage and retrieval system, including the Internet, without permission from the publisher, except in the case of brief quotations with proper citation in critical analysis or reviews.

ISBN: 978-1-4790-1010-3 (softcover)
       978-1-4790-1001-1 (hardcover)

Library of Congress Control Number: 2013950552

Printed in the United States of America

Year: 2013

Introduction

Music City Center, Nashville's large new convention complex, is a marvel, with its instantly recognizable, guitar-shaped curves; more than 8 acres of exhibit space; a $2 million art collection; and rolling roof, topped by a carpet of environmentally beneficial greenery. Convention planners will appreciate its 2.1 million square feet of space, parking for 1,800 vehicles and 57,500-square-foot Grand Ballroom, believed to be the largest in Tennessee.

But by the time Music City Center opened, it had become much more than just a building with lots of gee-whiz features. Though local officials had debated for years whether to construct it — and whether the city could afford its $585-million price tag — when the ribbon was cut on a bright spring day, Music City Center had become a symbol of Nashville's economic aspirations.

Politicians and financiers pressed ahead for construction despite a national recession. Hoteliers and restaurateurs view the center as a likely catalyst for a business boom, a magnet for conventioneers who will require everything from beds to barbecue. Developers expect Music City Center to spark a makeover of the South-of-Broadway neighborhood, which at the time of the complex's construction was a lackluster hodgepodge of adult entertainment, parking lots and eyesores.

Mayor Karl Dean predicted that the center will help grow Nashville's tourism business. "Today, we are not just opening the doors of a new downtown convention center, we are opening a new world of opportunity for Nashville's hospitality and tourism industry," he said. "Nashvillians are very much aware that we are on a positive trajectory in terms of moving forward. It's just a real positive thing for the city."

Music City Center's grand opening, on May 19, 2013, was accompanied by great fanfare. City officials estimated that more than 15,000 people came to explore downtown's newest landmark. Events, offered free to the public, included an open house, tours, children's activities in the exhibition hall and live music, including an outdoor concert headlined by rocker Sheryl Crow.

Like Nashville itself, Music City Center is bold and ambitious, proud of its personality and flair, and eager to flex its economic muscle. It is truly the city's showcase.

As visitor Nancy Vincent put it, "It's beautiful, and it's Nashville throughout, with the guitar ceiling and the classic framing. It meets up to the hype," she said. "This is the place you come see Nashville, and I think it's phenomenal."

These pages take readers inside Nashville's biggest civic building project and celebrate Music City Center's arrival.

Contents

The curtain rises on Music City's showcase 7

Art inside, greenery overhead 23

Behind the scenes, another world unfolds 33

MCC used to beguile conventioneers 39

A million nights by opening day 43

Art helps center sing 45

Songwriters' Hall finds a home 55

The muscle behind Music City Center 61

Construction 71

Omni adds Nashville flavor 75

Boom coming to SoBro 79

Landmarks in downtown Nashville 85

Tour info 91

The curtain rises on Music City's showcase

Naturally, Nashville opened its convention center with lots of music. But the real attraction was the stage itself, Music City Center.

Mikky Ekko performs during Music City Center's grand-opening concert. SHELLEY MAYS

Sheryl Crow headlines the free concert held for the public during Music City Center's grand opening. SHELLEY MAYS

The Time Jumpers, featuring Vince Gill, were among groups celebrating the center's opening. SHELLEY MAYS

Thousands of people showed up for festivities surrounding the center's official opening. SHELLEY MAYS

The Fisk Jubilee Singers, representing Nashville's Fisk University, perform during the center's grand opening concert.
SHELLEY MAYS

Mayor Karl Dean and members of the Metro Council cut the ribbon at the grand opening of Music City Center. JOHN PARTIPILO

MUSIC CITY'S SHOWCASE

People stream into the center after the ribbon cutting ceremony that formally opened the building.
JOHN PARTIPILO

"This is a big investment by the city and it took a lot of confidence in the city to make this investment during the recession. And I think it's going to pay off for us in a big way."

Mayor Karl Dean

ABOVE: Visitors pause by a view of the Country Music Hall of Fame and Museum and Nashville's Pinnacle building from Music City Center, on May 19, 2013. JAE S. LEE

OPPOSITE PAGE: Visitors stroll past entrances to exhibit halls during Music City Center's grand opening festivities. JAE S. LEE

A family steps into one of Music City Center's pop-out windows to explore the view. JAE S. LEE

Music City Center's green roof, planted with 14 types of vegetation, is designed to channel and conserve rainwater, cool the building and lower utility costs. DIPTI VAIDYA

PRECEDING PAGE: Soaring bowed windows, made of special low-iron-content glass to avoid a greenish tint, encase the Grand Lobby, sometimes called "the whale" for its curved sides. DIPTI VAIDYA

Balconies allow exterior views of the facility, such as this one, from several stories above ground level.
DIPTI VAIDYA

ABOVE: Natural light illuminates the west end of the exhibit hall. DIPTI VAIDYA

OPPOSITE PAGE: Pedestrians travel six city blocks if they walk the length of the building inside Music City Center. DIPTI VAIDYA

Architects Brian Tibbs, left, of Columbus, Ohio-based firm Moody Nolan; Seab A. Tuck III, of Tuck Hinton Architects, Nashville, center; and C. Andrew McLean, of tvsdesign, Atlanta; gathered for a pre-opening tour of the center on May 15, 2013. DIPTI VAIDYA

ABOVE: The Grand Lobby straddles Sixth Avenue, which runs through the center on street level, connecting Demonbreun Street with Korean Veterans Boulevard. The lobby also affords a view of much of downtown Nashville. MICHAEL BABIN

PRECEDING PAGE: The concourse offers a place to sit while enjoying a view of downtown Nashville. DIPTI VAIDYA

Music City Center officials claim the Grand Ballroom, with about 57,500 square feet, is the largest in Tennessee. It's equipped with a stage, and its guitar-shaped design creates many of the building's exterior curves. DIPTI VAIDYA

Columnar light fixtures glow from within over the Grand Lobby. DIPTI VAIDYA

Many balconies are tucked throughout the center to allow views both within and outdoors. DIPTI VAIDYA

Art inside, greenery overhead

"It's beautiful, and it's Nashville throughout, with the guitar ceiling and the classic framing. It meets up to the hype. This is the place you come see Nashville, and I think it's phenomenal."

Nancy Vincent, an early visitor to Music City Center

ART INSIDE, GREENERY OVERHEAD

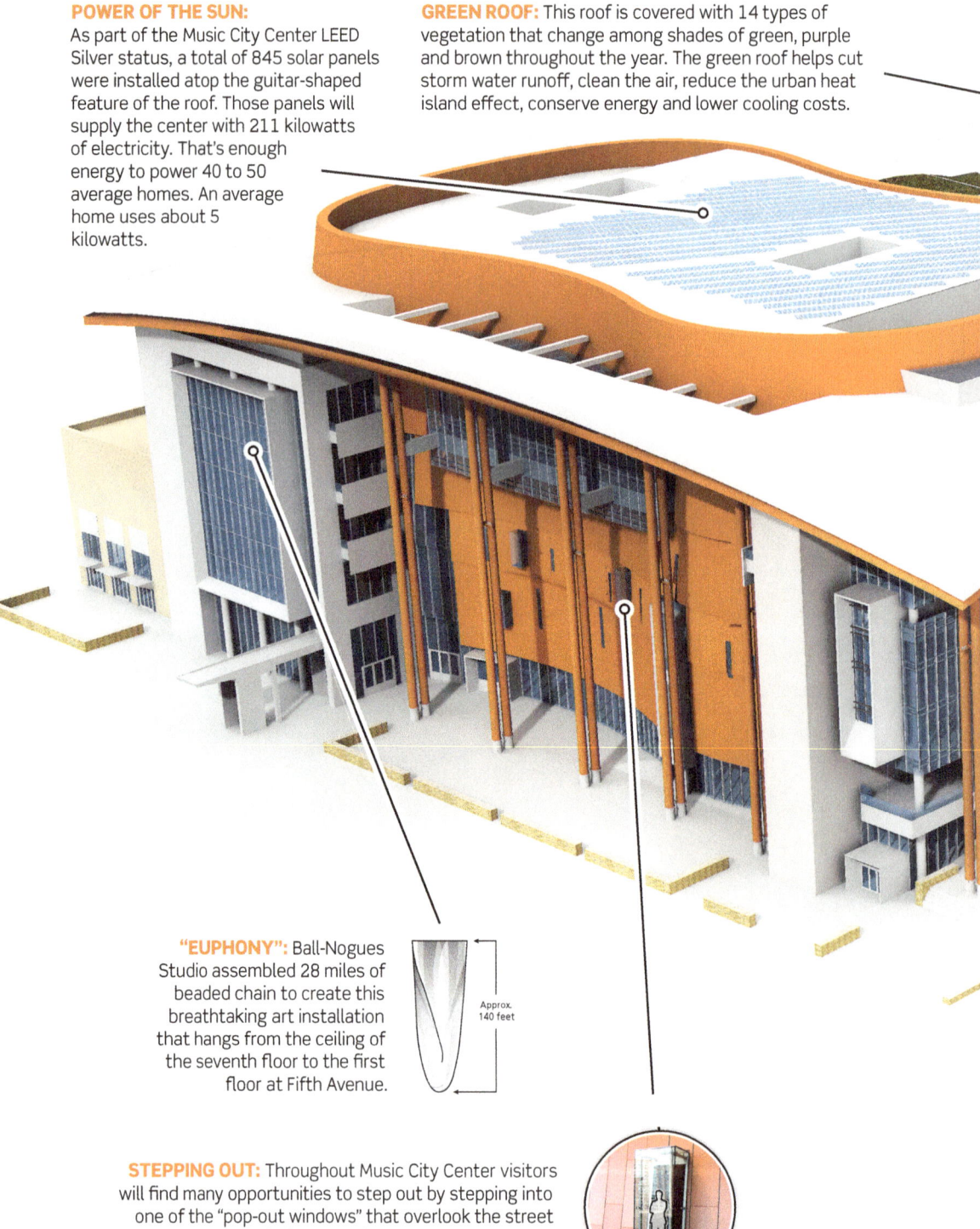

POWER OF THE SUN: As part of the Music City Center LEED Silver status, a total of 845 solar panels were installed atop the guitar-shaped feature of the roof. Those panels will supply the center with 211 kilowatts of electricity. That's enough energy to power 40 to 50 average homes. An average home uses about 5 kilowatts.

GREEN ROOF: This roof is covered with 14 types of vegetation that change among shades of green, purple and brown throughout the year. The green roof helps cut storm water runoff, clean the air, reduce the urban heat island effect, conserve energy and lower cooling costs.

"EUPHONY": Ball-Nogues Studio assembled 28 miles of beaded chain to create this breathtaking art installation that hangs from the ceiling of the seventh floor to the first floor at Fifth Avenue.

Approx. 140 feet

STEPPING OUT: Throughout Music City Center visitors will find many opportunities to step out by stepping into one of the "pop-out windows" that overlook the street below at various locations and levels.

MUSIC CITY'S SHOWCASE

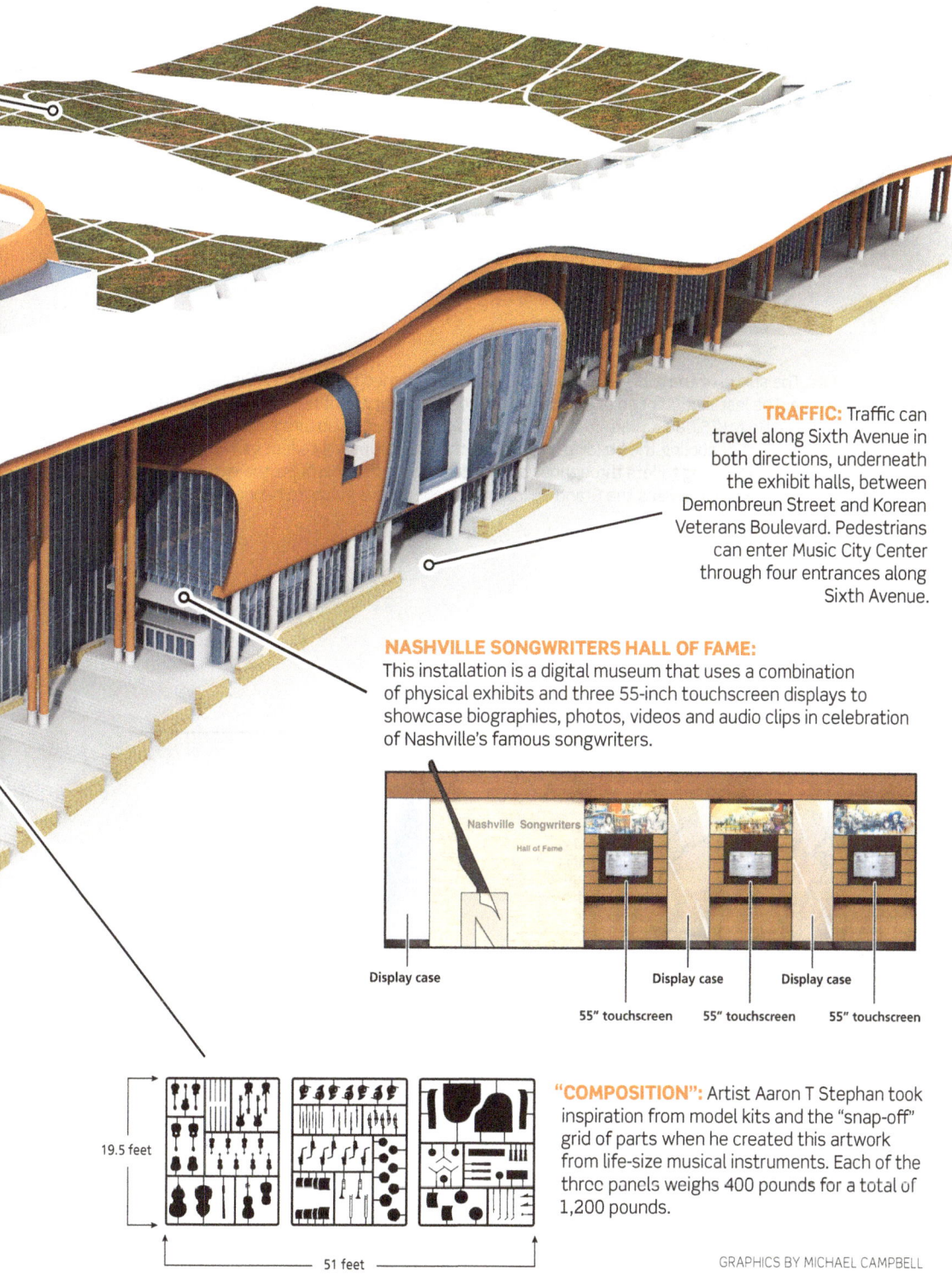

TRAFFIC: Traffic can travel along Sixth Avenue in both directions, underneath the exhibit halls, between Demonbreun Street and Korean Veterans Boulevard. Pedestrians can enter Music City Center through four entrances along Sixth Avenue.

NASHVILLE SONGWRITERS HALL OF FAME: This installation is a digital museum that uses a combination of physical exhibits and three 55-inch touchscreen displays to showcase biographies, photos, videos and audio clips in celebration of Nashville's famous songwriters.

"COMPOSITION": Artist Aaron T Stephan took inspiration from model kits and the "snap-off" grid of parts when he created this artwork from life-size musical instruments. Each of the three panels weighs 400 pounds for a total of 1,200 pounds.

GRAPHICS BY MICHAEL CAMPBELL

THE ROOF

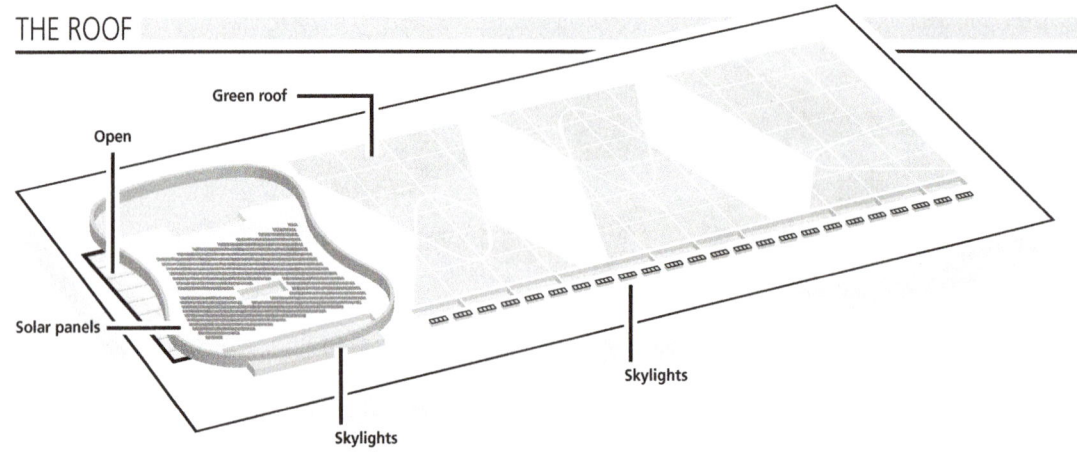

ROOF DESIGN: The shape of the roof, with its rolling hills, was designed to represent the rolling hills of Tennessee. The installation of solar panels will provide Music City Center with more than 200 kilowatts of electricity. A 175,000-square-foot "green roof" was installed to absorb heat from the sun and reduce the cost of cooling the building. In addition, the green roof will collect rainwater that will be stored for use in flushing toilets throughout the center and provide water for the exterior landscaping. The section that houses the Grand Ballroom is shaped like a guitar to honor Nashville's musical history.

LEVEL FOUR GRAND BALLROOM

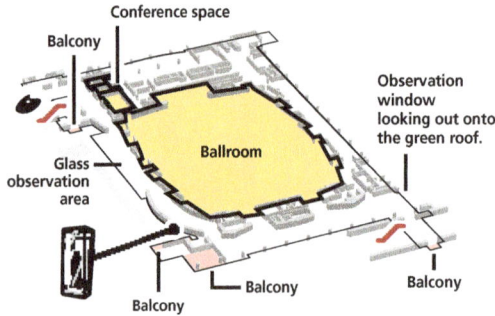

GRAND BALLROOM: The Grand Ballroom is designed to make you feel as if you were within a guitar. The ballroom can seat more than 6,000 people and is approximately 57,500 square feet. On this floor, visitors can enjoy the view and weather from four separate exterior balconies, or from the glass-walled pre-function area overlooking Fifth Avenue, or enjoy stepping into one of the "pop-out windows." Also, visitors can look out onto the green roof via the observation window.

■ Conference space   ■ Exterior balcony   ∫ Escalators   ● Art installation (large)

MUSIC CITY'S SHOWCASE

SHOW MANAGER OFFICES

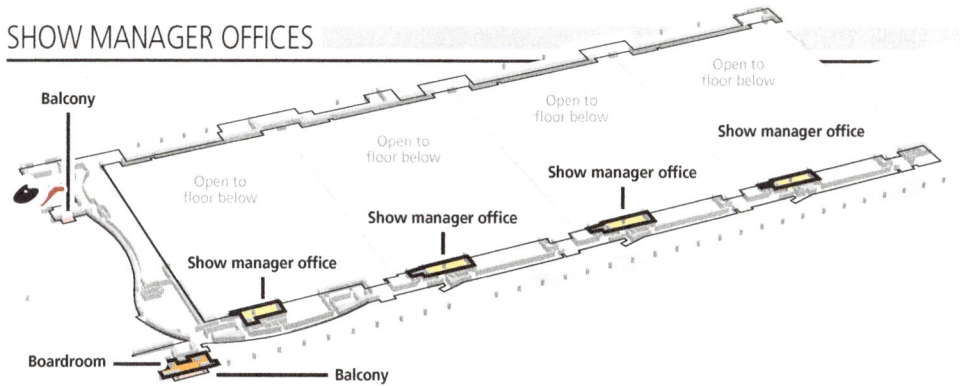

SHOW MANAGER OFFICES: There are four show manager offices that include a balcony and glass walls to overlook the exhibit halls on the floor below.

BOARDROOM: Attendees can have a board meeting while visiting the Music City Center. This boardroom has its own private exterior balcony.

LEVEL THREE EXHIBIT HALL

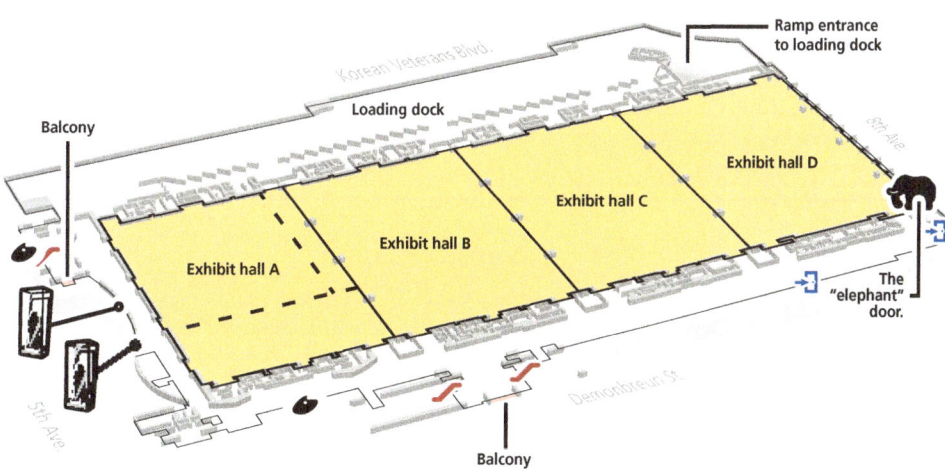

EXHIBIT HALL: The exhibit hall offers 350,000 square feet, more than 8 acres, of space. It can be divided into separate exhibit halls using sliding pocket doors and partitions. More than one mile of operable partitions. Room enough for up to 1,726 10-by-10-foot booths. Two "pop-out windows" that overlook Fifth Avenue. Long and wide enough to fit four 747s nose-to-tail along the length of the exhibit hall.

ENTRANCES: Two entrances, one from Demonbreun Street and the other from Eighth Avenue.

GRAPHICS BY MICHAEL CAMPBELL

ART INSIDE, GREENERY OVERHEAD

LEVEL TWO MEETING ROOMS

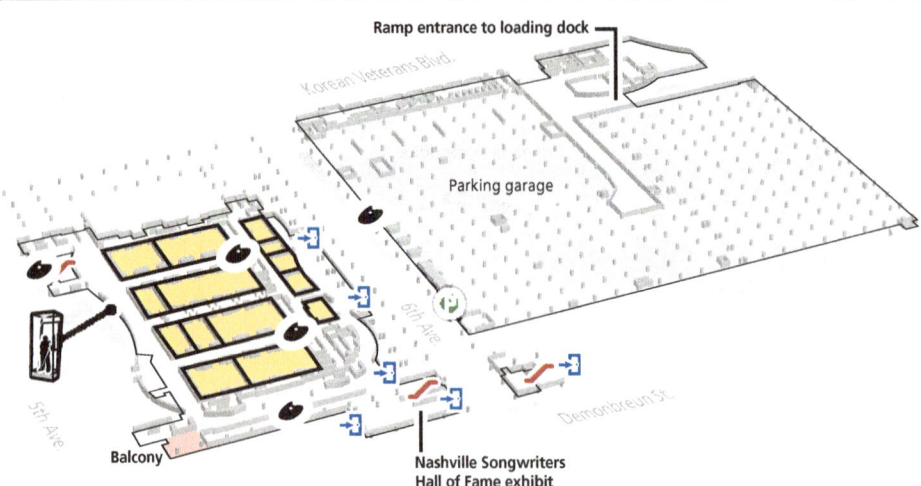

MEETING ROOMS: With 14 of them, some with the ability of being divided into additional space, this level offers 38,200 square feet of meeting space.

NASHVILLE SONGWRITERS HALL OF FAME: A display of memorabilia and three 55-inch touchscreen exhibits.

BALCONY: An exterior balcony overlooks the intersection of Fifth Avenue and Demonbreun Street.

ENTRANCES: A total of six on this level, four from Sixth Avenue and two from Demonbreun Street.

DAVIDSON BALLROOM

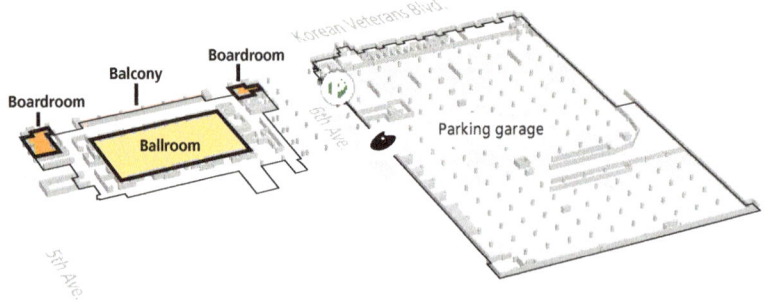

DAVIDSON BALLROOM: Can seat up to 1,500 people and is approximately 18,000 square feet.

BOARDROOMS: Two available on this level; both overlook Korean Veterans Boulevard.

BALCONY: An exterior balcony overlooks Korean Veterans Boulevard.

LEVEL ONE MEETING ROOMS

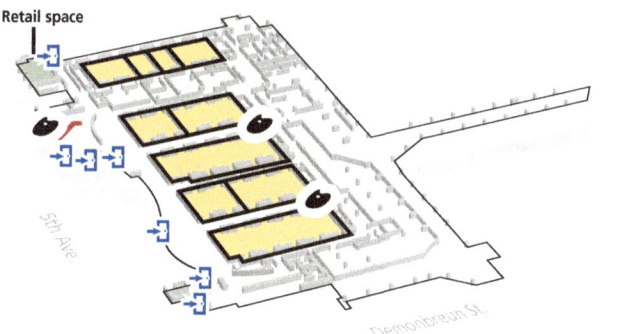

MEETING ROOMS: With 10 meeting rooms that can be divided into as many as 26 total rooms, this level offers a total of 41,850 square feet of meeting space.

RETAIL: A total of 5,000 square feet has been reserved for retail at the intersection of Korean Veterans Boulevard and Fifth Avenue.

ENTRANCES: A total of seven, six from Fifth Avenue and the seventh from Korean Veterans Boulevard.

Conference space   Entrance   Retail space   Escalators   Art installation (large)

GRAPHICS BY MICHAEL CAMPBELL

ART INSIDE, GREENERY OVERHEAD

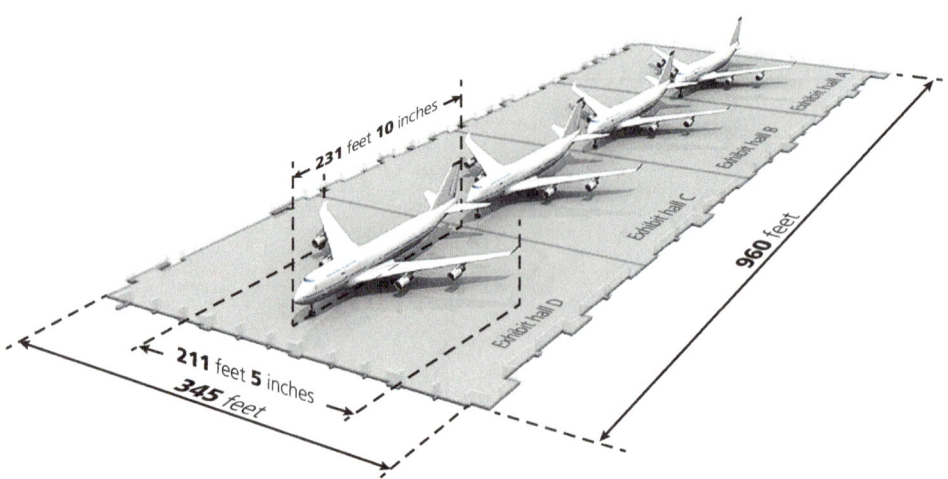

WHOA, THAT'S A LOT OF SPACE
With approximately 350,000 square feet spread across nearly 8 acres of space, there's enough room to park four Boeing 747s nose to tail. Note: There is room left over.

"ELEPHANT" DOOR
Along Eighth Avenue there is a freight door that opens directly onto the exhibit hall floor and is large enough to accommodate an elephant.

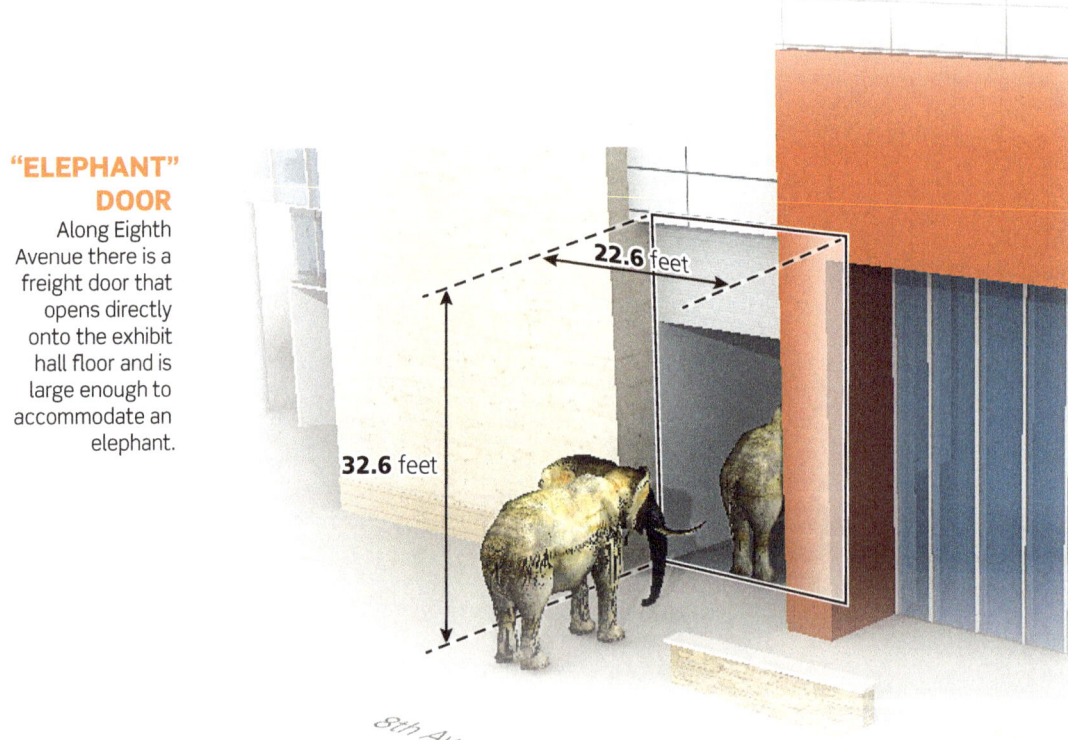

MUSIC CITY'S SHOWCASE

EXHIBIT SPACE
Comparison of the exhibit hall square-footage of the Nashville Convention Center with that of the Music City Center.

☐ **Nashville Convention Center**
■ **Music City Center**

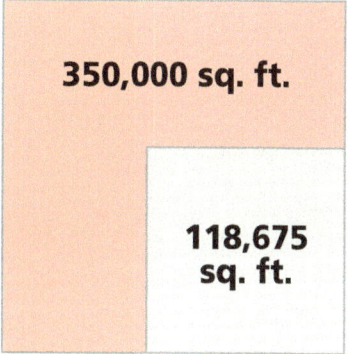

CONCRETE USED IN CONSTRUCTION
In the construction of Music City Center, 110,000 cubic yards of concrete were used. Compare that with the construction of LP Field, where 56,000 cubic yards of concrete were used.

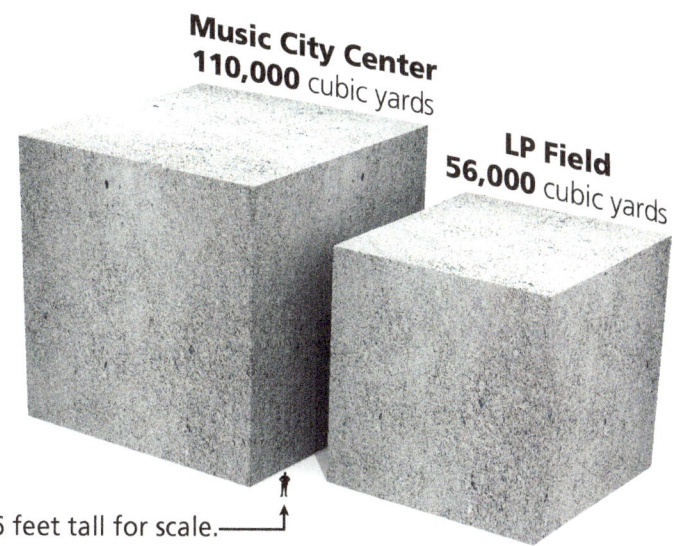

A person standing at 6 feet tall for scale.

GRAPHICS BY MICHAEL CAMPBELL

Behind the scenes, another world unfolds

By G. Chambers Williams III

The ballroom is decorated to look like a Hawaiian island, with waterfalls and a smoking volcano. Next door, the banquet hall has 5,000 people sitting at tables, all of them eating steaks. In the exhibit hall, 300 booths are set up to display a variety of goods, brought in by a fleet of tractor-trailer trucks. Out front, a line of buses waits to shuttle convention guests to hotels and shopping or sightseeing venues. And waiting in the wings — mostly out of sight of event attendees — harried meeting planners and coordinators keep their fingers crossed, hoping all goes well after months of careful planning and preparation culminating in the bustle of a typical convention or conference.

The kitchen in the newly constructed Music City Center. DIPTI VAIDYA

That's just one possible scenario for how a large convention might play out, creating an entirely plausible but massive to-do list.

"It's almost like a Titans football game on Sunday," said Charles Starks, director of Nashville's Music City Center. "We do a lot of work on Monday, Tuesday, Wednesday, Thursday and Friday getting ready for a few hours on Sunday afternoon. Only for us, it's months in advance, not just a few days."

That's the world of putting together a major convention, he said, and there is so much going on behind the scenes that most people have no clue about. His staff alone numbers 150 people, but with contractors and other outsiders involved, successfully planning and executing a large event often takes 1,000 workers or more.

Half of Music City Center's 2.1 million square feet of space lies where the public never goes.

Cooks Teresa Gosse, left, and Ruben Ortega work in Music City Center's kitchen. DIPTI VAIDYA

"You do have to take the planning seriously. If you've got 6,000 people to feed, you don't just run out to Kroger and buy 6,000 steaks."

– Music City Center President and CEO Charles Starks, on the facility's capacity for serving enormous crowds, with features such as kitchen freezers large enough to accommodate forklifts

Music City Center's "elephant door" can accommodate an elephant — and more importantly, trucks hauling convention materials. MICHAEL BABIN

"That includes kitchens, where we have coolers and freezers big enough to drive forklifts into and out of," Starks said. "The typical big convention or trade show will have 200 to 250 trucks come in with exhibits and such, and when a show is going on, moving in or out, there might be a couple hundred people behind the scenes just setting up or tearing them down."

Food is always a challenge, but one that convention centers are set up to handle, Starks said.

"It's all in the planning, and if you take care of the little details, the big things will fall in place," he said. "But you do have to take the planning seriously. If you've got 6,000 people to feed, you don't just run out to Kroger and buy 6,000 steaks."

CHOREOGRAPHING SERVICES

An event that involves a lot of people must be well choreographed, just like a stage production, said Rhonda Marko, owner of Destination Nashville, a "destination management" company that organizes events and carries them through.

"We work with the meeting planner, and once they select a hotel, we provide everything the hotel does not provide," Marko said.

Her firm provides or coordinates necessities such as transportation, decorating, catering, security, audiovisual, entertainment, team-building exercises, tours and so forth, she said.

"We're the conduit between the meeting planner and all of the vendors and venues in the city," she said.

With all of these resources available, the new Music City Center can handle a heavy workload, Starks said.

"By the time we're up and going well, we will do 230 to 240 events a year," he said. "We'll see maybe 35 to 40 large convention and trade shows a year. And we want to have a lot of small stuff to fill in around when the big shows aren't here. We hope to keep it busy year-round."

"We talked about food and philosophy and so on. I really fell in love with the project. I found out (Music City Center CEO Charles Starks) wanted to do a great job in putting Nashville on the map as far as convention centers ...

He also said he wanted to hire as much as possible locally with products that are from a radius of about 200 to 250 miles. All that he said was things I was already doing in my previous positions as a chef.

For me, I have on my resume as a footnote: I want to be a good steward to the food, the land, the sea, the community, the people and my colleagues. I believe in that."

Max Knoepfel, Music City Center Executive Chef, recalling his job interview

MCC used to beguile conventioneers

By Jaquetta White

The 21st floor of the Pinnacle office building is Butch Spyridon's canvas. From the cavernous space, with its floor-to-ceiling windows offering a panoramic view of downtown Nashville and beyond, the president of the Nashville Convention & Visitors Corp paints a picture for any groups that are considering holding conventions in Music City.

"All of this was well thought out to be as convenient as possible," Spyridon said to a group from the American College of Gastroenterology on a clear day in late April 2013 as he waved an arm before them and gestured toward the Music City Center, Omni Nashville Hotel, Bridgestone Arena and Country Music Hall of Fame and Museum on the ground below. "All of that is a real compact package."

As Music City Center has gone from a hole in the ground to a steel frame to an actual building, Spyridon made the trip to the 21st floor with increasing frequency. The bird's-eye view of the city has become a staple of the tours given to prospective conventioneers.

FOCUS ON DOWNTOWN

The tours are one of several ways the sales staff of the CVB has set about tackling the task of filling Nashville's massive new meeting hall, which can hold three times as many attendees as the Nashville Convention Center, making the new facility a viable option for larger groups the visitors corp has never before been able to woo. The CVC also has tripled the size of its sales team and changed its pitch to focus more on the downtown corridor.

"This is the first time we're looking at Nashville," said Bradley Stillman, executive director of the gastroenterology group, on the morning of his visit to the city. The association was considering bringing 5,500 medical professionals and exhibitors to town in 2020 for an annual conference and exhibition.

At a minimum, the medical group needs a space large enough to hold at least 3,000 people in a classroom-style setting, Stillman said. Nashville has never been a contender for the annual meeting because it didn't meet that basic requirement. Stillman and the other group members were certain the MCC would meet that need.

But they traveled to town to make sure there are enough hotel rooms close to dining and entertainment options that association members could enjoy the trip.

CVC President Butch Spyridon, left, in April 2013 talks with Bradley Stillman, Elaine McCubbin and Dan Jones of the American College of Gastroenterology, about holding the group's 2020 annual meeting at Music City Center. GEORGE WALKER IV

"The less they have to get in a cab to do, the more likely we are to use (a city)," Stillman said.

That's where the CVC team came in.

"You're going to get the 30,000-foot view of the city and us and the future," Spyridon told the group of three as it embarked on a full day of meetings and tours that included Music City Center and models of the guest rooms then under construction at the Omni and Hilton hotels.

INTEREST BURGEONING

Visits from groups such as Stillman's tripled from about four a month when Music City Center broke ground to 12 per month by spring of 2013. Such visitors are invited by a more robust sales team of 16, up from 10 before the center's groundbreaking.

The visits often focus more heavily on downtown, a departure for the Nashville Convention and Visitors Corp, which once considered that area a liability.

"Before, it was primarily a Gaylord message," Spyridon said, referring to Gaylord Opryland Resort and Convention Center, east of downtown. "Downtown was secondary. It's a completely different market set now. It's been nice to put the city out front."

That shift has made Nashville more attractive to groups such as Stillman's.

"We're seeing a much more diverse group of meetings — more medical, more professional, more corporate," Spyridon said, though early groups making use of Music City Center also included Music City Sports Festival, the CMA Music Fest 2013's Fan Fair, and the National Association of Music Merchants.

Stillman said he found Nashville "impressive." The group wasn't yet ready to award the medical conference to the city when it left town. There were other sites to visit and consider. But, for the first time, Nashville was part of the conversation.

"Music City Center will likely have more economic impact than any other major development project in the city's history."

Butch Spyridon, president of Nashville Convention & Visitors Corp

A million nights by opening day

By Joey Garrison

He waited until the very end, but Butch Spyridon met his goal. Before the Metro Council's 2010 vote to bankroll Tennessee's most expensive municipally financed project, the president of the Nashville Convention & Visitors Corp made a pledge: By the time Music City Center opened, there would be more than 1 million nights booked in Nashville hotel rooms as a result of future conventions and trade shows. According to Spyridon, he first announced the 1-million-nights goal at a council presentation to sway votes: "I got up, and put something out there that lets everybody know how serious we are."

For project boosters, it became the primary way — arguably, a symbolic one — to measure the center's progress. And on May 20, 2013, the day of the center's ceremonial opening, Mayor Karl Dean announced that hotel-room bookings had crossed the threshold. The updated figure in mid-May: 1,062,787 room nights and 123 events.

"To me, this is a complete vindication of the strength of Nashville as a destination," Dean said at the ribbon cutting for the $585-million center.

Some of those bookings occurred just days earlier, he added, highlighting one of the groups that put the city over the magic number. Shriners International will hold one meeting at Music City Center and another at Gaylord Opryland Resort & Convention Center, east of downtown in Donelson. "You can't beat that," Dean said.

The moment made for a perfect punctuation to celebrate a facility that tourism officials pushed for more than a decade — a building for which it started to book events even before Metro acquired all the property needed to build it.

Conventions that helped push Music City Center past the long-standing goal include: Distributive Education Clubs of America (DECA), generating a combined 62,000 room nights in 2016 and 2020; Church of God International, bringing 18,900 room nights in 2018; and a group remaining confidential, which will bring in 34,580 room nights for an event in 2021 (the most of any one convention).

Official say the 2.1 million-square-foot center was necessary to attract larger groups to town – for example, the National Rifle Association's national convention in 2015.

"There is no building seeing this kind of activity prior to opening," Music City Center CEO Charles Starks said.

Art helps center sing

By Jim Myers

While many convention centers can be dull, utilitarian spaces, like blank canvases waiting for a corps of conventioneering dental hygienists to come decorate the darkness with dancing toothbrushes, Nashville's new Music City Center is a showpiece in and of itself. From its undulating roof, an instant landmark in the skyline, to the grand ballroom, which will make conventioneers feel like Jonah in the beautiful belly of one whale of a guitar, the center's architecture elicits all kinds of wows.

Nashville artist Dane Carder has three pieces, each 6 feet tall, on display at Music City Center. They're based on photographs he took during a reenactment of the Battle of Shiloh in March 2012, the 150th anniversary of the battle. SARAH B. GILLIAM

Carder, pictured here in his studio, is among 52 artists whos work is displayed at Music City Center. Of those, 48 hail from Tennessee. SARAH B. GILLIAM

"Euphony" is a delicate curtain, created from a total of 25 miles of metal chain and flowing 117 feet – four stories – from the ceiling from an elliptical ring. Its airy look is deceiving; the work weighs 3,500 lbs.
DIPTI VAIDYA

Planners and designers took the showplace theme one step further by earmarking $2 million for the purchase of art. That commitment to the yards of walls and open spaces will further help define Music City Center as a metropolitan showpiece.

The Metro Nashville Arts Commission helped design the committee structure, selection process and call for proposals. For the eight commissioned pieces that are site-specific, the committees received more than 221 proposals from artists all over the country. In the end, two Nashville artists, Jamaal Sheats and Fisk University art professor Alicia Henry, joined a cadre of five others from Los Angeles to Portland, Maine, to create works that in some cases are on a scale as massive as the center itself.

One such piece, "Euphony," by the Ball-Nogues Studio in California, connects 25 miles of colored stainless steel chain that drapes and folds like a diaphanous vortex, dropping 117 feet from the ceiling in one of the site's tallest open spaces.

Along the open Sixth Avenue corridor running through the building, Bob Zoell created a mural of painted tiles that artistically spans the four seasons along 135 feet. His stark graphic style and recognizable rectangular-bodied birds have been chosen for seven New Yorker magazine covers throughout his long career.

On a smaller scale, if you can call 21 panels that cover a 21-by-9-foot space small, Henry explores intimacy and peace in her stark but textural study in white and black.

That scope of scale was one of the great challenges confronting the committees selecting the artists, and for the consultants, Rich Boyd and Brian Downey, who were tasked with choosing and installing the pieces.

In addition to the commissioned pieces that were created to fill very specific spaces, 2,500 images, the result of a call to artists within a 250-mile radius of Nashville, were narrowed down to what was essentially an approved shopping list of artists.

More than 60 pieces by 48 Tennessee artists were acquired to help add interest to the walls that line the convention space corridors, and the work is a testimony to the breadth and quality of the creative community in and around Middle Tennessee.

During a tour, Downey talked about how the works along the five primary corridors were loosely grouped by themes, such as mixed media, figurative art, paper and landscapes. Fans of the local photography scene also will appreciate works by Bob Schatz and Bob Delevante.

While the artists were not required to weave in themes of music, many did, in surprising ways. The scale and style of the architecture drove some of the design, and moved Aaron T Stephan, one of the commissioned artists, to create a giant floating orchestra. The instruments, all in white, are connected to three aluminum frames by small spurs, a design inspired by model car kits where each part comes attached to a plastic grid — only in this case the grid is 51 feet long.

OPPOSITE PAGE: Aaron T Stephan's creation, titled "Composition," is a network of musical instruments. Stephan was inspired by toy model kits, in which parts come attached to a plastic grid, when he designed his music-themed "Composition." DIPTI VAIDYA

Another playful take on local lore is a series of four painted panels by Tim Hooper, honoring Davy Crockett, Minnie Pearl, Johnny Cash and sculptor William Edmondson. A study of the Crockett painting gives some insight into Hooper's sense of humor. In the painting, a hatless Crockett casts a sharp eye toward a wayward raccoon. To his side sits a leather satchel with two books, and you can't help but chuckle when you read the titles: "Frontier Fashions" and "Hats for Men."

There are also technological marvels, like the laser-cut wood panels of Christie Nuell, a former Middle Tennessee State instructor who retired to the Isle of Man, or Charles Clary's hand-cut paper designs climbing a wall near one of the many staircases.

Visitors curious about a piece or its artist can learn details by using a smart phone to scan the QR code mounted on the wall next to each work of art. The code routes background information about the work to the smart phone, making Music City Center a tech-savvy, user-friendly art gallery in addition to a world-class convention hall.

The $2 million designated for these works is a small part of the budget that created Music City Center, but it's a huge commitment to local art, and to making the convention center a true destination.

AT RIGHT: Artist Brad Sells created "Rachel's Garden: Hermitage Series #51" from burled sugar maple. He said that a tree "humbles me with its soulful, timely patience, thriving and dying at the same time." MICHAEL BABIN

OPPOSITE PAGE: "Flameobic Opulation" is a wall-mounted cluster of small colorful towers made of hand-cut paper, by Charles Clary. The artist was born in Morristown, Tenn., and by 2013 lived in Murfreesboro, Tenn. DIPTI VAIDYA

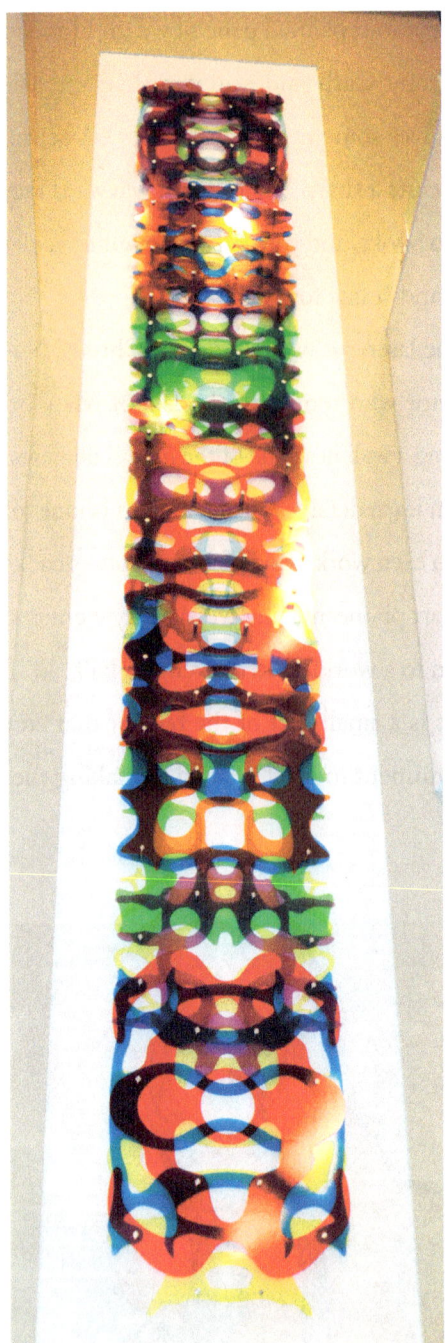 

Phillip K. Smith III created two colorful pieces for Music City Center. This first (above left), called "Chladni," is 32 feet tall and mounted at the east end of the center in the meeting room corridors. It's named for Ernst Chladni, who nearly 200 years ago mapped sound patterns. The second piece (above right) is titled "Spectrum II." Its colors fluctuate as the viewer moves around the work. SHELLEY MAYS

Bob Zoell's mural depicts Nashville's skyline and the four seasons, incorporating whimsical images of weather and music in a 165-foot-long display along Sixth Avenue, which runs through the center. On this day in April 2013, the building was nearing completion. SHELLEY MAYS

Artist Jane Braddock, one of dozens of local artists whose creations are displayed at the center, works at her Nashville studio. Three of her paintings, named for the Greek gods Apollo and Zeus and the goddess Artemis, hang in the center. Braddock's notes on the Music City Center website mention that she liked tying the names of the paintings to Nashville's nickname as the "Athens of the South."
SARAH B. GILLIAM

Nashville artist Jamaal Sheats, pictured here, was one of two Nashville artists who won commissions to create large-scale art for Music City Center. Fisk University art professor Alicia Henry is the other.
SARAH B. GILLIAM

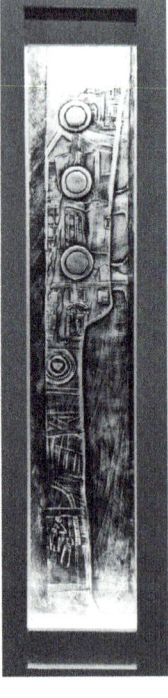

Sheats created "8 Octaves". It includes eight metal panels with a musical theme.
SARAH B. GILLIAM

Songwriters' Hall finds a home

By Cindy Watts

It's not the freestanding museum on Music Row they once hoped for, but songwriters agree that the exhibit dedicated to the Nashville Songwriters Hall of Fame at Music City Center is far more than they could have dreamed of even three years ago. "You have to think about it in terms of a whole," said songwriter Pat Alger, chairman of the Nashville Songwriters Hall of Fame. "On one hand, it's not a standalone museum or anything like that. But, it is a state-of the art digital museum."

The songwriters hall of fame includes touch-screen technology that lets visitors listen to popular songs while reading about the writers who created them. MICHAEL BABIN

Displayed prominently in the area of Music City Center facing Sixth Avenue and Demonbreun Street, the new Nashville Songwriters Hall of Fame exhibit is a wall that's 10 feet high and 50 feet long.

Three wheelchair-accessible touch-screen computers are mounted on the wall, which also houses display cases for memorabilia. The touch screens are interactive, with all the members' names alphabetized on the screen. Guests choose a name and that songwriter's catalog is displayed along with song clips, photos and possibly videos or lyric sheets.

Ken Paulson, vice chair, left, and songwriter and chairman Pat Alger visit the Nashville Songwriters Hall of Fame, built into Music City Center, on May 10, 2013, days before the center's opening.
SANFORD MYERS

Songwriters are honored with their names carved in stone in the Nashville Songwriters Hall of Fame.
DIPTI VAIDYA

The exhibit continues outside the building with an area called Songwriters Square, where members hope they will one day host songwriter events. The square is inlaid with stones inscribed with the names of all 188 Nashville Songwriters Hall of Fame members, the year they were inducted and their songs. Members' song titles also are engraved on the stairs leading into the building.

"On paper, it sounds modest, but when you see it, it's really cool-looking, I think," Alger said. "The stone work outside is the ingredient I really like. (Inside), I like to say the money is behind the wall."

"This is a very important part of the life in Nashville, especially from a music perspective, and it needed a good home. Music City Center is such a new, iconic part of the city — then what better place to have the home of the Songwriters Hall of Fame than inside the center?"

Marty Dickens, Chairman of the Convention Center Authority

Songwriter Bobby Braddock signs his autograph on a board during the press conference announcing the Nashville Songwriters Hall of Fame location at Music City Center, on Oct. 4, 2012. JAE S. LEE

IT STARTS WITH A SONG

Several Nashville Songwriters Hall of Fame members attended Music City Center's grand opening to meet visitors and chat about their songs: Bill Anderson ("Tips of My Fingers" and "Whiskey Lullaby"), Bobby Braddock ("He Stopped Loving Her Today" and "Time Marches On"), Alger ("Small Town Saturday Night" and "Unanswered Prayers") and Don Schlitz ("The Gambler" and "Forever and Ever Amen").

Marty Dickens, chairman of the Convention Center Authority, said having the Hall of Fame exhibit inside the center benefits both the songwriters and the 1.2-million-square-foot complex. The hall's exhibit brings an authenticity to Music City Center that is uniquely Nashville, and its location puts the exhibit in front of thousands of people daily, thus raising awareness of the hall and its members.

"This is a very important part of the life in Nashville, especially from a music perspective, and it needed a good home," Dickens said. "Music City Center is such a new, iconic part of the city, then what better place to have the home of the Songwriters Hall of Fame than inside the center? I think it's going to do so much for the hall. I think it's a great partnership."

The exhibit marks the first time in the hall's more-than-40-year history that the organization has had a permanent place to call home. For the songwriters who have been inducted, it makes their membership seem more real.

"We were in the Hall of Fame, but not really, because we weren't anyplace except on a piece of paper at a ceremony and getting our picture taken," said Braddock, a member of both the Country Music Hall of Fame and the Nashville Songwriters Hall of Fame. "It was a portrait with no place to put it, but now they have that."

Anderson, a member since 1975, couldn't agree more or be more excited about the exhibit.

"We've all heard it all begins with a song, and then it seems like the songwriters get left out," he said. "I think this is such a wonderful way to do it, and it's taken so long. I remember sitting in those board meetings 30 or 40 years ago saying, 'We need a place to do this.' I don't think anyone dared to dream when we finally got one that it (would) be as great as this one is going to be."

The muscle behind Music City Center

By Getahn Ward

More than 7,300 workers and 400 contractors brought Music City Center from the drawing board to reality. The task of coordinating the construction of the largest municipal project in Nashville history fell to three men: Gary Schalmo of Clark Construction Group, Kevin Keller of Bell & Associates Construction LP and Don Hardin Jr. of Harmony Construction Group LLC. Each man brought skills and expertise to the project. But beyond skills, the three men said the time and effort it took to get people from different companies and backgrounds to work together efficiently were the keys to success.

GARY SCHALMO
FOCUS ON SAFETY

Gary Schalmo. LARRY McCORMACK

Schalmo said bringing the construction management team aboard early when the architect was being hired was important, because it gave the builders a voice during the design process. "You're starting to see that more and more on these larger jobs," he said.

Schalmo said the project's scope is on a scale all its own. When the concrete was being poured, for instance, he once saw a monthly invoice from a contractor that topped $20 million.

He's proudest of efforts to ensure that the project's safety program was followed closely. For instance, construction companies quickly put a requirement in place that workers had to wear gloves at all times after they observed fingers getting cut.

The building's height and unique shape created logistical challenges, Schalmo said, citing the extra time and planning required to get materials, including pre-assembled structural steel trusses, to the roof or various levels. "We're basically a 15-story building, even though when you go inside you only see four or five levels," he said. "Each level is so tall."

"We're basically a 15-story building, even though when you go inside you only see four or five levels."

DON HARDIN JR.
RECRUITING LABORERS

Hardin, whose firm had a hand in finding laborers, recalled challenges identifying local contractors who could perform certain tasks at the level required for such a massive project. He credits outreach efforts, including pairing smaller companies with larger ones. The aim: to surpass a goal of spending 20 percent of the construction budget with minority- and women-owned small businesses. With roughly 130 such businesses involved, the result was closer to 30 percent, officials said.

One recruiting effort featured an on-site trailer that helped screen potential workers who were then assigned to different subcontractors. "It saved a lot of companies the time and the overhead it takes to go out and find people and do interviews," Hardin said.

Don Hardin Jr. LARRY McCORMACK

Hardin has enjoyed seeing many of the construction workers on the building project get hired for jobs with the convention center. "We know the building is definitely going to impact a lot of jobs," he said. "You're also going to see ... some places that are dormant aren't going to be dormant for long."

"We know the building is definitely going to impact a lot of jobs."

KEVIN KELLER
'YOU'LL REALLY BE AMAZED'

Kevin Keller. LARRY McCORMACK

Keller said he never fully stopped marveling at the massive structure, which spans six city blocks. "The public has looked and driven by it, but wait until you get inside and see this thing," he said. "You'll really be amazed."

The project also had its share of distractions, including a protest by a group that beat paint-bucket drums with sticks to bring attention to its cause. "It got on your nerves, but we certainly weren't going to let them know it at the time," he added. "And ... without comments or anything to them, they finally quit beating on their drums."

Keller expects the convention center to continue serving as an economic engine as hotels and other developments pop up in the area south of Broadway. "It was a terrible time in the economy," Keller recalled of the period before construction began in 2010. "Certainly, this gave the local economy a boost and put a lot of people to work."

"The public has looked and driven by it, but wait until you get inside and see this thing."

COORDINATED EFFORT

The project required:

35,000 square yards of woven carpet

110,000 cubic yards of concrete

16,500 light fixtures

13,000 tons of steel

1,100 doors

480 miles of electric conduits

60 miles of plumbing

Visitors can access different levels through *22* elevators and escalators

The parking garage can accommodate *1,800* cars

Ryan Garcia, superintendent for Conti Electric, moved to Franklin from the West Coast to work on Music City Center. SANFORD MYERS

RYAN GARCIA

Ryan Garcia, superintendent for Conti Electric, worked on larger jobs ranging from solar projects to hotel casino high-rises. He came from Las Vegas and Los Angeles to work on Music City Center, which he called "a historic event for Nashville."

"I'm proud of the projects I've worked on and what I've done. I don't solicit people and tell them I did that, but I'm proud of what I've done. Finishing is gratifying."

Robin Giltner, of Clarksville, attended Vanderbilt University. In September 2011 he was superintendent of mechanical, electric and plumbing for Bell/Clark on the Music City Center project. SANFORD MYERS

ROBIN GILTNER

Robin Giltner worked as superintendent of mechanical, electric and plumbing for Bell/Clark for the project until November 2012, when he accepted a job as the center's engineering manager, overseeing electrical, mechanical, plumbing and sprinkler operations.

"I hope to stay until I retire. I've never been part of a project and then stayed afterward, so I'll be looking at it through a different set of eyes. It's something Nashville can say is the only one of its kind."

THE MUSCLE BEHIND MUSIC CITY CENTER

Ron Page is a plumber who worked on Music City Center with Foley Co. SANFORD MYERS

RON PAGE

Ron Page is a plumber with Foley Co. through the local union No. 572. The Mt. Juliet resident worked on Music City Center for nearly three years.

"The convention center is going to bring a whole lot to Nashville. Not just as far as just tourism, but also in the building trade, because along with the convention center, you have all the hotels starting to pop up. ... To look at it from outside, it looks big, but once you are on the inside, it's just huge."

Bobby Phillips is among the Music City Center construction team members intending to continue working at the center now that it's opened. SANFORD MYERS

BOBBY PHILLIPS

Bobby Phillips operated the sweeper and managed cleanup crews during Music City Center's construction. He was working in South Carolina when he applied for a job on the project. His truck broke down coming back on his interview day. Phillips didn't arrive until that evening, but he persisted in getting his interview and landed the job. He expects to stay on the center, working on the grounds and in maintenance.

"I've been here three years. You put a lot into it, and it's something to be proud of. ... I'm glad I'll be around to take care of it."

Mark Sturtevant is no stranger to enormous construction projects. SANFORD MYERS

MARK STURTEVANT

Mark Sturtevant, Metro Convention Center Authority's project and development manager, has worked on many of Nashville's largest building projects, including LP Field, Bridgestone Arena and the Farmers' Market.

"This is the biggest, this and the football stadium. It's a good feeling ... you become personally invested. It kills me when I hear someone criticize the project. I don't know that it's been different (from other projects), but this one has gone very smoothly. Mostly because of the people. It's a really good team across the board."

Construction

"It is enormous. It's breathtaking how big it is. You walk in and — those high ceilings. You're like 'wow.' I think it's pretty safe to say that, even given what we do every day, that's a pretty large facility."

Donald Orr, president of Nashville Machine Co., which installed Music City Center's elevators and escalators

ABOVE: Fireworks erupt during the center's groundbreaking ceremony, on March 22, 2010.
LARRY McCORMACK

LEFT: Mayor Karl Dean, center, congratulates Music City Center Authority Chairman Marty Dickens, left, as Butch Spyridon, president of the Nashville Convention & Visitors Corp looks on during Music City Center's groundbreaking ceremony.
LARRY McCORMACK

MUSIC CITY'S SHOWCASE

ABOVE: Three years before Music City Center opened, its future site, pictured here on May 19, 2010, was little more than a field of dirt, dotted with earth-moving equipment, across the street from the Country Music Hall of Fame and Museum. MANDY LUNN

RIGHT: Mark Alvarez runs a power saw in August 2010 during the center's construction. JAE S. LEE

CONSTRUCTION

Artwork festoons construction fencing surrounding the Music City Center construction site in February 2012. SAMUEL M. SIMPKINS

The center's swooping roofline takes shape in January 2013, rising in the skyline against the AT&T building in the background. SHELLEY MAYS

Ceco Concrete Construction General Superintendent Frank Brazzale signs a beam during a "topping out" ceremony on Jan. 19, 2012. That's a construction-industry tradition, held when the highest beam of a structure is ready to place. More than 1,000 workers autographed the uppermost Music Center Center beam and enjoyed a free lunch in one of the center's ballrooms. Mayor Karl Dean attended and thanked workers for their efforts.
SANFORD MYERS

Omni adds Nashville flavor

By Getahn Ward

A guitar-shaped lobby, Hatch Show prints in each room, a restaurant serving Southern cuisine and a honky-tonk should give guests staying at downtown's new Omni hotel the Nashville feel. In addition, a connector linking Music City Center's anchor hotel to the Country Music Hall of Fame and Museum will allow visitors to become immersed in Music City history without even going outside. The connector is part of the museum's $100-million, 210,000-square-foot expansion, which includes a new entrance off Fifth Avenue South, additional space for exhibits and a new education center.

ABOVE: Window washers clean the southern façade of the Omni hotel in July 2013, a few months before the 800-room luxury hotel planned to open. SAMUEL M. SIMPKINS

OPPOSITE PAGE: The Omni hotel, scheduled to open Sept. 30, 2013, will grace its rooms with Nashville-themed art. GEORGE WALKER IV

Linking the buildings should create opportunities to co-market to conventioneers and museum attendees, said Jan Freitag, senior vice president at lodging research firm STR in Hendersonville. "It creates a win-win situation for both the Omni and the Country Music Hall of Fame."

The Country Music Hall of Fame expects at least a 25 percent increase in visitors from its overall expansion, said its director, Kyle Young. Adjacent to the museum's new lobby off Fifth Avenue South will be multiple retail spaces, including one for Hatch Show Print, a production area where the prints will be made, the new Haley Gallery and a restaurant.

Omni strives to give the luxury hotel, under construction since June 2011, a Nashville flavor. In addition to the Southern-style three-meal Kitchen Notes

The eastern end of Music City Center allows an up-close view of the Country Music Hall of Fame and Museum's expansion, and construction of the Omni Hotel, with its rooftop pool, progressing across Fifth Avenue in August 2013. MICHAEL BABIN

Omni Nashville Director of Sales and Marketing Tod Roadarmel said in spring 2013 that he expects the Omni hotel in Nashville to have one of the strongest openings in company history. GEORGE WALKER IV

restaurant and honky-tonk Barlines, the 800-room hotel will have a Bob's Steak and Chophouse, Bongo Java coffee shop and Mokara, which it bills as downtown's only full-service spa.

In mid-August 2013, the hotel was some six weeks away from opening, with nearly 700 employees and nightly room rates ranging from $199 to $399. Six months before the scheduled opening, on April 5, 2013, it exceeded its goal of booking a quarter-million room nights. Those reservations extend into 2024, company officials said. According to Tod Roadarmel, Omni Nashville's director of sales and marketing, "It will be one of the most successful openings in our company's history."

Boom coming to SoBro

By Josh Brown

Shawn Courtney had one word to describe Nashville's SoBro neighborhood when he opened his restaurant there in 2006: "gnarly." The area south of Broadway stretching between the Cumberland River and Interstate 40 had a reputation for adult entertainment establishments and run-down buildings and as a hangout for the city's homeless. "Basically you had small rickety buildings and parking lots," said Courtney, who owns the restaurant Past Perfect, on Third Avenue South. "It just looked like that area of town that was just kind of abandoned. It was dark. There were not a lot of lights."

Economic development officials hope the South of Broadway neighborhood, seen here from Music City Center, will sprout gleaming new buildings, especially hotels. MICHAEL BABIN

In the time since Courtney opened his eatery, however, a tide of new development has turned around the neighborhood, bringing popular restaurants, entertainment and tony new office buildings.

With the opening of Music City Center, city leaders are expecting SoBro to continue its momentum, remaining the city's development hot spot for years to come.

"Music City Center is going to change the center of gravity," said Barry Long, CEO of Pittsburgh-based Urban Design Associates, which the convention center hired to study the neighborhood and create a master plan. "When it opens, I think you're going to see a change in the economy for all of South of Broadway."

The master plan is one of two studies released since December 2012 offering a glimpse of the potential of the SoBro neighborhood in coming years. A second

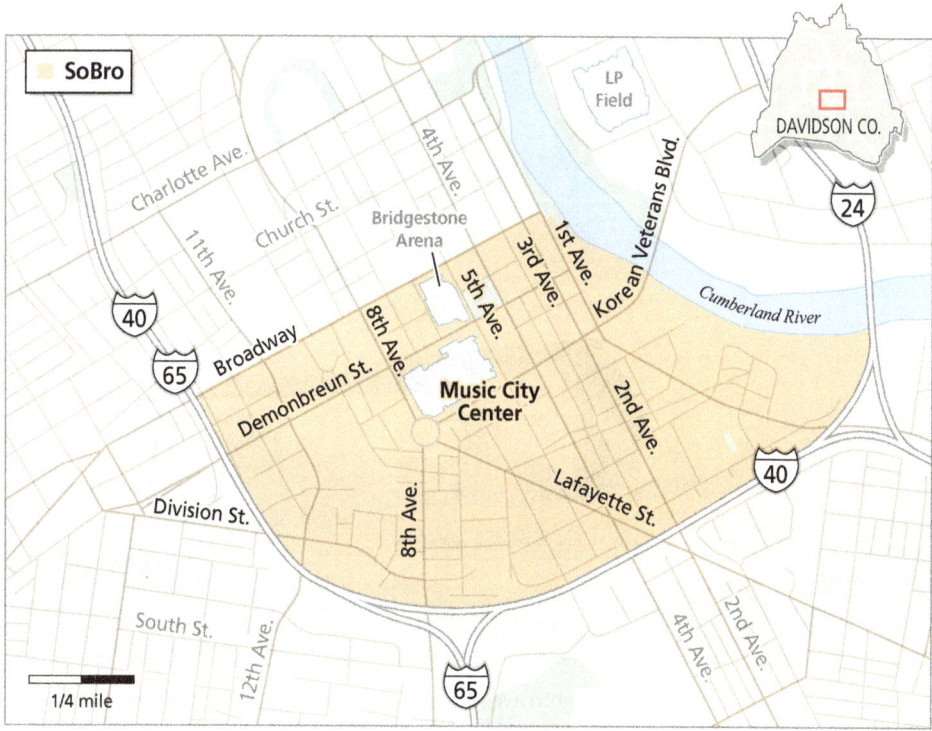

THE TENNESSEAN

analysis of overall development in downtown Nashville envisions thousands of new hotel rooms to serve conventioneers, a growing demand for homes and stores in the area, and hundreds of thousands of feet of new office space — with much of that demand centered in SoBro.

Randall Gross, director of Washington, D.C.-based Randall Gross/Development Economics, which performed the market analysis for the Metropolitan Development and Housing Agency, said the development of the new convention center has gotten the attention of the real estate community in a way that few other projects could.

"The convention center has increased the exposure of SoBro, and sort of put it on the map as a place where development is happening," Gross said. "Developers want to be there because of the exposure of the convention center and the changes that are happening."

Motorists navigate the intersection of Eighth Avenue and Korean Veterans Boulevard next to Music City center through a roundabout constructed in tandem with the project. MAURA AMMENHEUSER

The convention center's impact has come first in the form of new demand for hotel development. The Omni Nashville Hotel is scheduled to open in the fall of 2013 with 800 rooms adjacent to Music City Center, and by mid-2013, more than 1,000 additional rooms were under construction or planned for the area.

Still, Gross estimated that hundreds more hotel rooms will need to be constructed within walking distance to meet convention center needs.

"There is still additional demand for large blocks of rooms and full-service hotels," Gross said. "There are hotels under construction in the West End corridor, and some of those will have shuttles to downtown. But it isn't ideal. Convention planners would like to have the hotels within a 15-minute walk of the center."

TRYING TO MEET DEMAND

By early 2013, there were signs that some hotel developers and commercial real estate investors were attempting to meet that demand.

"It seems like every week someone is announcing a new hotel down there," said Tom Frye, managing director at commercial real estate firm CB Richard Ellis in Nashville.

By July 2013, 14 new downtown hotels — six next to the center — were either under construction, going through the permit process or had been announced, accounting for 3,450 new rooms on top of Nashville's existing 24,828 rooms.

Among the most recent announcements: plans for a full-service, 450-room, $135 million Hyatt Regency on Broadway at Third Avenue; and a 400-room, $120 million Marriott across from Music City Center on Demonbreun Street, between Seventh and Eighth Avenues.

"That people are actually buying land, building buildings — they're not taking a risk because of a study," said Bert Mathews, president of Nashville-based The Mathews Co., which develops, owns and manages commercial real estate properties.

As more hotels move in, the demand for restaurants and entertainment also grows.

"If you think about what people do when they come into town for a convention: entertainment and restaurants," Frye said. "You'll see growth in an already well established entertainment base."

That's already happening, he said: "You can already see the restaurants starting to line up."

He pointed to eateries such as Etch and The Southern, already operating in SoBro.

Gross' market analysis found demand for an additional 531,000 square feet of retail and entertainment space in downtown Nashville by 2017. Of that, he estimated that 41,000 square feet will be for restaurants and bars.

"SoBro could capture a substantial share of this demand, particularly in dining and entertainment potential generated in large measure by Music City Center traffic and tourism growth," Gross wrote in the report.

Shawn Courtney opens the windows on a bright day in November 2012 at Past Perfect, his restaurant on Third Avenue South. JOHN PARTIPILO

A DRAW FOR RESIDENTS

Ultimately, the dream of many of the city's planners and real estate developers is to see the neighborhood nourish a vibrant residential community.

While the convention center doesn't have a direct impact on housing, the restaurants and entertainment that serve conventioneers also appeal to residents.

"If those amenities exist, it makes the whole downtown more attractive," Gross said.

For Past Perfect owner Courtney, SoBro has already come a long way from the early days of his business, and he hopes the convention center will mean more business.

"Maybe this will be a good way to transition ourselves from that Music City-Broadway-honky-tonk thing to a more well-rounded area," he said. "I think it's just another reason to come here."

Landmarks in downtown Nashville

Music City Center joines a long list of iconic structures defining Nashville's skyline.

The legendary stage for country music and performers of all genres, and the former home of the Grand Ole Opry, Ryman Auditorium stands at 116 5th Avenue North. JAE S. LEE

ABOVE: Union Station opened on Broadway in 1900 to serve booming railroad traffic in Nashville. Today it's a luxury hotel. JAE S. LEE

OPPOSITE PAGE: The state capitol building, at 600 Charlotte Ave., dates to 1859. LARRY McCORMACK

LANDMARKS IN DOWNTOWN NASHVILLE

A full moon sets behind the Life & Casualty tower, right, as the sun rises on March 28, 2013, casting a warm morning glow over the Nashville skyline. The AT&T building is at left. LARRY McCORMACK

The Nashville Convention Center is Nashville's first convention hall. It sits across Broadway from Bridgestone Arena and across Fifth Avenue North from Ryman Auditorium. LARRY McCORMACK

The Life & Casualty Tower, opened in 1957 by the Life & Casualty Insurance Co., was Nashville's first skyscraper. It stands at 401 Church St. RICKY ROGERS

The Country Music Hall of Fame lies across Fifth Avenue South from Music City Center. It attracts hundreds of thousands of visitors annually. GEORGE WALKER IV

The Schermerhorn Symphony Center is home to the Nashville Symphony. DIPTI VAIDYA

The NHL Predators play at the Bridgestone Arena. The arena is also a venue for countless concerts and other shows every year. JAE S. LEE

LP Field is home to the NFL's Tennessee Titans. Originally called Adelphia Coliseum, it's pictured here in September 2001. JOHN PARTIPILO

Tour info

Music City Center offers free public tours of the facility on approximately a weekly basis, for a maximum of 25 people. Tours last 45 minutes to an hour and require a lot of walking. Visitors must register for a tour in advance by choosing a date on the Music City Center website. For more information, see the website at: www.nashvillemusiccitycenter.com

NEXT PAGE: Music City Center glows against Nashville's lights on the evening of April 25, 2013, a few weeks before its grand opening. DIPTI VAIDYA

CREDITS

"Music City's Showcase" was produced by the staff of The Tennessean:

Maria De Varenne, Executive Editor and Vice President/News
Meg Downey, Managing Editor
Deborah Fisher, Senior Editor/News
Knight Stivender, Director/Audience Engagement and News Marketing
Lance Williams, Business Editor
Tom Stanford, Visuals Editor
Maura Ammenheuser, Book Production Editor
Michael Babin, Design Team Leader
Michael Campbell, Graphics Design
Ricky Rogers, Photo Researcher

Reporting staff: Josh Brown, Nancy DeVille, Joey Garrison, Jim Myers, Getahn Ward, Cindy Watts, Jaquetta White, G. Chambers Williams III

Photography staff: Frank Empson, Sarah B. Gilliam, Jae S. Lee, Mandy Lunn, Shelley Mays, Larry McCormack, Sanford Myers, John Partipilo, Ricky Rogers, Samuel M. Simpkins, Dipti Vaidya, George Walker IV

Editing staff: Heather Fritz Aronin, Alice Baldwin, Brian Belt, Misty Emery, Craig Flagg, Lisa Green, Jonathan Houghton, Jim Keutzer, John Mitchell, Jamee Smith, Jeff Walter

Digital media staff: Todd Barnes, Karen Grigsby, Karen Kraft, Michael McCann, Eric Stromgren, David Yunker

CPSIA information can be obtained at www.ICGtesting.com
Printed in the USA
LVOW02*0612071113

360350LV00002B/3/P